YOUR BIRTHDAY

A SURVIVAL GUIDE

BY MARTIN BAXENDALE

Published by Silent But Deadly Publications,
21 Bisley Road, Stroud, Glos. GL5 1HF, U.K.

ISBN 0 9522032 3 5

Printed in the U.K. by Stoate & Bishop Ltd,
Cheltenham, Glos.

CONTENTS

INTRODUCTION

Birthdays can be a hazardous and traumatic time, especially as the years start to add up and you begin to dread that "special" day coming around again...and again...and again...

The worry and the depression as you contemplate yet another year flown past all too quickly...

Yet another birthday looming ahead, and with it, those ever-increasing signs of advancing age - a new grey hair here, an extra wrinkle there; an ever-more outmoded and embarrassingly laughable taste in music; a strange new fondness for bizarrely-patterned wooly cardigans, comfortable slippers and a hot milky drink at bedtime...

And can you still cope with the physical stresses and strains of what in your younger days you were able to take in your stride; like the marathon birthday booze-up and the titanic after-birthday hangover, the nerve-racking birthday party chat-up and the non-stop all-night birthday bonking session?

Yes, without this invaluable and comprehensive BIRTHDAY SURVIVAL GUIDE by your side, these and countless other birthday worries can so easily turn your happy day into THE DAY FROM HELL.

THE BIRTHDAY BLUES

A common problem with numerous possible causes, which may strike without warning at any time as the Happy Day draws near, or on the Day itself.

Can range from a bit fed up, through vaguely pissed-off or mildly depressed, to hopeless doom-laden despair and dire suicidal desperation.

WARNING SIGNS:

Watch out for the following give-away signs of a fast-approaching bout of Birthday Blues:

Irresistible urge to scream "SOD OFF, YOU BASTARD!!" at people who ask how old you'll be this year.

Wimpering pitifully "Oh God! Oh God! Oh God!" as you sit and stare woefully at the calendar, mentally ticking off Your Last Few Days Of Not Being Incredibly Old And Decrepit.

An inability to look in a mirror without screaming in abject horror and lurching desperately towards the nearest bottle of hair colour, tube of anti-wrinkle cream or do-it-yourself plastic surgery kit.

NOTE: The Birthday Blues of course tend to be most severe when you hit the "biggies" (30s, 40s, 50s etc). The following psychological chart (compiled after exhaustive study and thorough medical research) gives a rough indication of what you can expect:

30 - Mildly fed-up in a general over-the-hill-ish, past your 'best-before' date, sort of way.
40 - Middle-aged panic and hopeless hysteria, doom, gloom and despair sort of thing.
50 - As 40, plus "Oh, God! Where did my hair/teeth/chin/waist/sex-life go to?!!!"
60 - As 50, plus imminent retirement staring you in the face: "Finished! On the scrap-heap! Useless! A burden on society! For pity's sake, SOMEONE SHOOT ME! PLEASE!!!"

HOW TO AVOID WORRYING ABOUT THOSE UNWELCOME SIGNS OF ADVANCING AGE

A) Take down all mirrors in your house/flat at least a fortnight before birthday.

B) Paint over all mirrors with black paint.

C) Paste onto mirrors blown-up photos of you when you were younger.

D) Wear paper bag over your head when looking in mirrors.

(B)

(A)

(C)

(D)

Of course, another dead give-away sign of aging is actually starting to like all those naff presents that elderly relatives always give you, like ghastly patterned socks, wooly cardigans and crap aftershave/cheap perfume.

For the sake of appearances, always be sure to sneer and take the piss, even when you secretly quite fancy that horrendous pair of tartan slippers or fuchsia-pink bed-jacket.

HOW TO AVOID SIGNS OF ADVANCING AGE

HOW TO AVOID WORRYING ABOUT PEOPLE FORGETTING YOUR BIRTHDAY

The simple answer to this common cause of the Birthday Blues is to drop a few subtle hints.

LOOKING BACK AND FEELING SORRY

Birthday Blues can also be caused by looking back over the year and regretting what you've done or not done, achieved or not achieved.

Whatever you do, for God's sake DON'T go phoning your 'ex' or 'exes', regretting that acrimonious split-up; not when you're suffering from the Birthday Blues and emotionally vulnerable; and certainly not on your birthday when you're pissed as a fart and don't know what you're saying or doing.

Past mistakes are difficult enough to live with, without going and making them all over again. (See also 'Embarrassing Situations' and 'The Morning After').

THE BIRTHDAY BOOZE-UP

The birthday booze-up/birthday party can prove to be an extremely hazardous situation fraught with potential dangers and distasteful consequences.

The greatest hazard is, of course, that of getting so rat-arsed pissed that you end up making a total prat of yourself (see also 'Embarrassing Birthday Situations') and/or suffering from the Mother Of All Hangovers (see also ' The Birthday Morning-After').

Best possible advice is to (a) Have a proper meal and/or get stuck into the party grub before you start on serious exercising of your drinking elbow. (b) Don't mix your drinks. (c) Watch that your mates don't spike your drinks. And (d) take care not to have that 'one too many'.

Now you will remember that, won't you? Of course you will.

TAKE CARE NOT TO MIX YOUR DRINKS

BEWARE SPIKED BIRTHDAY DRINKS

Spiking your drink is one of the commonest birthday booze-up pranks.

WARNING: By the end of the evening your drink may have been spiked so many times that it could be virtually 99% vodka or Pure Polish Spirit, and just 1% whatever you were drinking in the beginning.

This can prove a serious fire/explosion hazard. As the evening progresses, take care to keep your glass well away from naked flames and if possible avoid smoking and drinking at the same time.

Cut out this sticker and fix to your glass towards the end of the evening.

One precaution you can take against the danger of seriously spiked drinks is to have a taster with you on the Birthday Booze-up.

Someone especially sensitive to and easily inebriated by spiked drinks is advisable (e.g. Granny, baby brother or sister, small domestic pet, etc).

This is also useful for detecting and warning of so-called mates playing other pranks with your drinks, putting 'funny-baccy' in your roll-ups, or introducing humorously revolting foreign objects and substances into your party snacks and/or late-night curry.

Beware so-called mates taking your glass to the bar for a birthday refill, by way of the toilet.

IF GOING FOR A LATE-NIGHT BIRTHDAY CURRY, TAKE NECCESSARY PRECAUTIONS

EMBARRASSING SITUATIONS

Birthdays are rife with potentially embarrassing situations and dire consequences, especially during and as a direct result of the birthday booze-up/birthday party.

Major hazards to be especially wary of include: Birthday pranks played on your by your so-called mates; people finding out just exactly what your real age is; and a limitless range of excrutiatingly embarrassing situations of a sexual nature, often not un-connected with over-indulgence during the birthday booze-up.

Indeed, as the following few pages clearly demonstrate, it is probably advisable to completely avoid that major pitfall the birthday bonking session.

The embarrassment potential of this particular situation is truly astronomical, given all the usual prevailing (alcoholic) circumstances and the subsequent high probability of unfortunate mistakes and ego-destroying failures.

BIRTHDAY PRANKS

Some of the most embarrassing birthday situations result from pranks played by so-called mates; usually involving things like forcible removal of clothing, luminous paint, handcuffs and railings in public places, or the sudden appearance of embarrassing Birthday Strip-a-grams, etc. (See also 'Spiked drinks' in section on Birthday Booze-up).

SURPRISE STRIP-A-GRAMS CAN PROVE HIGHLY EMBARRASSING

BEWARE! Surprise birthday pranks can come in all shapes and sizes. Be especially wary during the birthday booze-up of any unusual-looking birthday gift packages and odd-looking situations.

The simplest defence against birthday pranks (especially twats who want to give you your 'birthday bumps') is to hire yourself a thunking great Birthday Duff-a-gram to duff up anyone who even thinks about playing silly buggers with you on your special day.

THE BIRTHDAY PARTY CHAT-UP

When you're a bit 'tired and emotional' in the middle of the Birthday Party/Booze-up is the worst time of all to practice your chat-up lines.

Given the likely levels of inebriation/stonedness, your judgement is sure to be slightly impaired.

It is advisable therefore to have within your Birthday Party group a 'nominated non-drinking bloke/bird fancier' who can steer you safely away from your less advisable choices of snogging/bonking partners.

NOMINATED NON-BOOZING BLOKE/BIRD FANCIER

Cut out this badge and attach to a nominated non-boozing bloke/bird fancier in your party or birthday booze-up group.

AVOIDING UNWELCOME BIRTHDAY KISSES

HANDY HINT: A quick immitation festering cold sore can be easily assembled and stuck onto your lip, using a small lump of party pizza topping and a blob of avocado dip; guaranteed to put-off the most amorous of unwelcome birthday snoggers.

IF NO-ONE GIVES YOU A BIRTHDAY SNOG

It can be highly embarrassing if, in the course of an entire evening partying, not a single solitary person (or domestic pet) feels the urge to give you a birthday snog.

Not to worry. Simply nip upstairs to the bedroom, where you will of course have the vacuum cleaner hose ready to give yourself a convincing fake love-bite, which you can then strut around the party and show off to your heart's content.

WARNING: Don't get carried away in the bedroom. You'd be surprised just how many people end up in casualty every year following sexual experiments with vacuum cleaner hoses.

WHEN EVERYONE DISCOVERS JUST EXACTLY WHAT YOUR REAL AGE IS

Not a lot you can do really. Serves you right for inviting your Mum, Dad or other Elderly Relative to the birthday party. It's almost always them who give the game away (and give you all those naff patterned socks/wooly cardigan/crap aftershave/cheap perfume birthday gifts too).

Seems a shame that they're the very people you can't possibly keep your birthday a secret from.

'EX' MARKS THE SENSITIVE SPOT

Phoning your 'ex' or 'exes' when you're 'tired and emotional' at Birthday time doesn't just bring the risk of regretting previous split-ups and repeating old mistakes.

Inviting your 'ex' to the birthday party/booze-up can also lead to numerous other embarrassing birthday situations.

For example, your 'ex' may well take the opportunity to kick you when you're emotionally 'down', especially if you later manage to 'pull' and end up with a new partner in the course of the evening.

Your guests may be highly amused and entertained by your ex's voluble recollections and reminiscences of your sexual peculiarities and inadequacies, but you and/or your new partner won't be.

IF EVERYONE FORGETS YOUR BIRTHDAY

One of the worst possible birthday nightmares. You plan a huge party, buy in gallons of booze and tons of party grub, invite everyone you know.........and no-one comes.

But don't sit around moping. What's important is to make everyone think that loads of people came. Always have ready a selection of life-size carboard cut-outs of party-goers. Draw curtains and place cut-outs with bright lights behind to give impression of a full house.

Turn music up full blast or, better still, play back at top volume tape-recording of the last late-night party racket from next-door or the flat upstairs, which kept you awake into the small hours (authentic sound effects and revenge too).

If the odd guest or two should turn up eventually, late in the night, greet them cheerfully at the door with the sad news that the local fire chief has declared the party so crowded that fire regulations won't allow any more guests in.

THE MORNING-AFTER

Naturally, if you've been a sensible birthday boy/ birthday girl then you'll have taken care not to over-indulge during the birthday booze-up, and you'll be feeling fresh as a daisy the morning after.

You'll also have been careful to avoid, while befuddled with drink, leaping into bed with the first person (or domestic pet) to use his or her tongue when giving you your birthday kiss.

You'll have politely thanked all your party guests for their lovely presents, tidied up and washed the glasses, and gone to bed early with a book and a hot milky drink.

Yes of course you did. So here are some hints on how to cope with that hangover, make your excuses and generally sort out the revolting, nauseating mess that is the squalid, festering residue of your 'special day'.

THE BIRTHDAY HANGOVER

Hangover cures come in two basic varieties, the coffee-and-aspirin regime, and the hair-of-the-dog (see illustrations). On health grounds we would strongly recommend the first, but the second variety has obvious appeal to the more serious piss-artists among us and, let's face it, can be much more fun.

HANGOVER CURE NO. 1

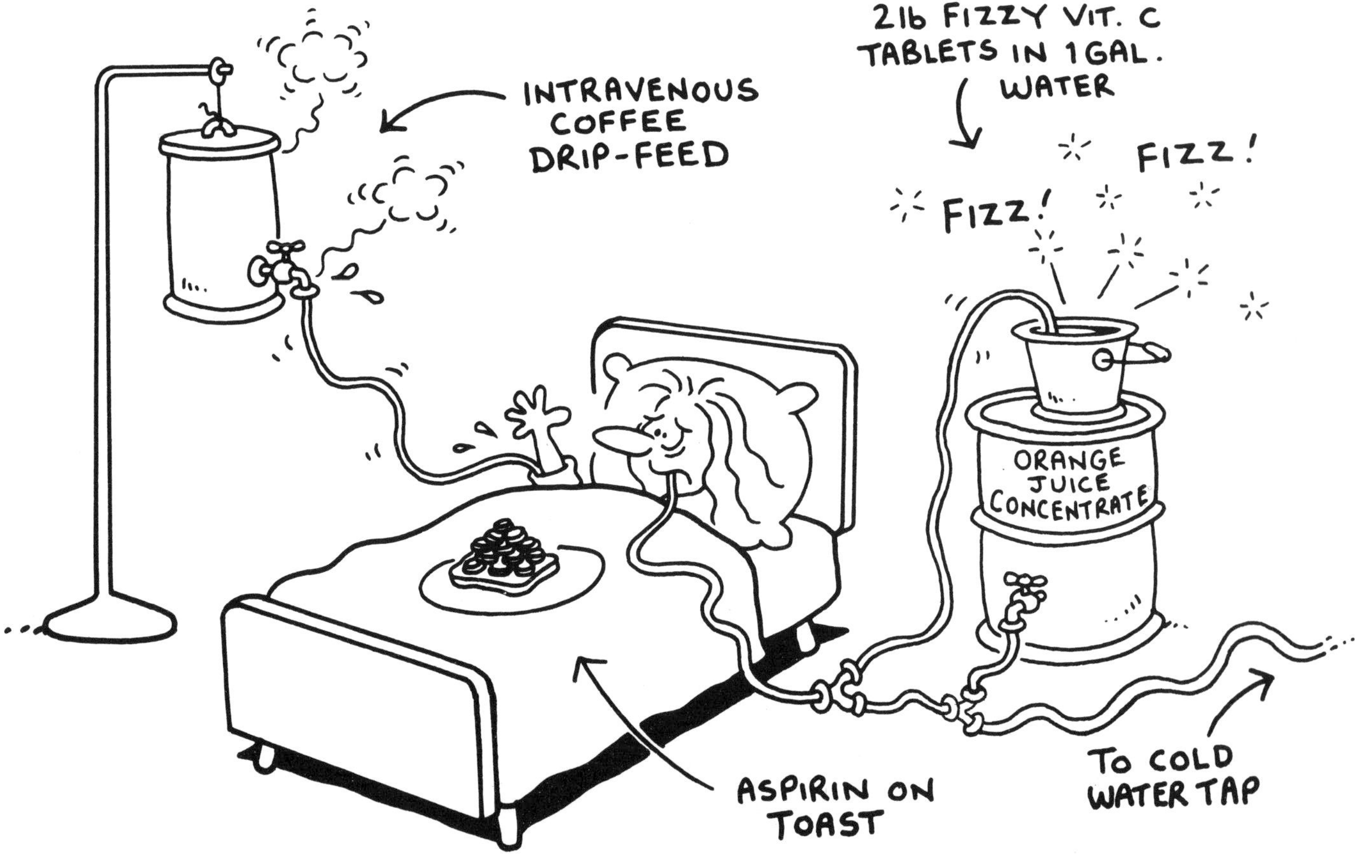

HANGOVER CURE NO. 2

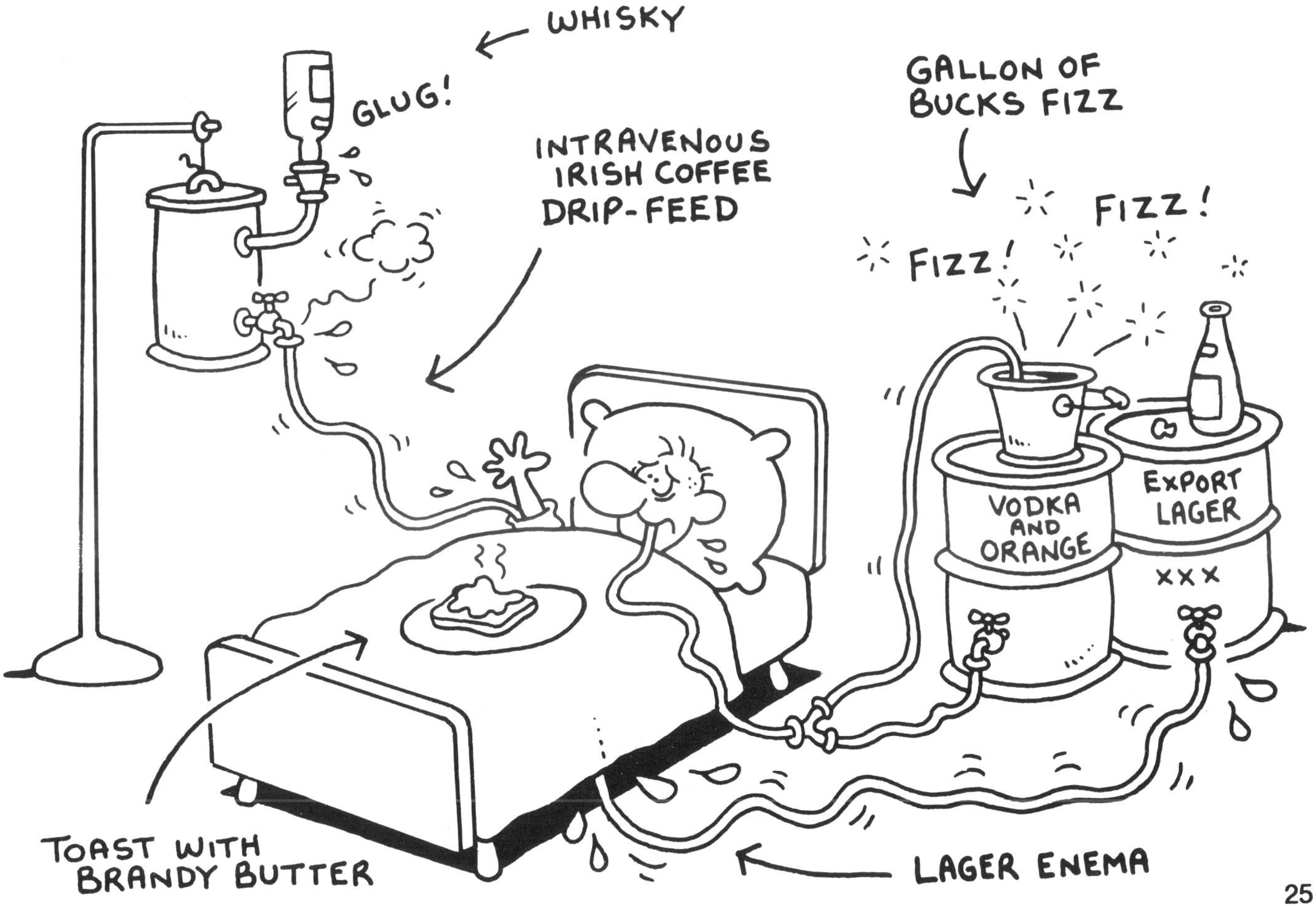

Apart from feeling like shit, you'll find that the after-birthday hangover poses another major problem if it occurs on a workday: Whether to struggle into work and suffer quietly all day, or stay in bed watching daytime TV and playing with yourself. Duh, difficult choice, huh?

Okay, so here are some handy tips on how to make your "calling in sick" telephone excuses to the boss sound more convincing.

MAKING IT SOUND LIKE YOU'VE GOT A BAD COLD, RATHER THAN JUST A HANGOVER, WHEN YOU CALL IN SICK TO WORK:

Useful aids for making you sneeze, cough and sniffle convincingly on the phone include: Pepper pot, pipe full of old navy shag tobacco, tear gas, CS gas, etc.

MAKING IT SOUND LIKE YOU'VE GOT SEVERE FOOD POISONING, RATHER THAN SIMPLY A HANGOVER, WHEN YOU CALL IN SICK.

Hot-water bottle full of cold custard: A useful aid for making it sound like you have the 'runs'. For best effect, use while phoning from bathroom (on a cordless or mobile phone) followed by frantic high-speed whizz of loo roll and repeated loud flushing.

WAKING UP WITH SOMEONE YOU WOULD NORMALLY RUN A MILE TO GET AWAY FROM

In this situation, we recommend making your excuses in an honest but sensitive and caring way, something on the lines of:

"I'm really very sorry, but I think we've both made a big mistake here, and...Owch! Christ that hurt! Hey! What're you doing with my clothes and those scissors?!!!"

WRITING YOUR 'THANK YOU' NOTES

All well-brought-up birthday boys and birthday girls should sit down the next day and write lots of 'thank-you' notes to everyone who gave them presents and who came to the party.

Then sit down with your diary and a list of your friends' and relatives' birthday dates, and plan your revenge on all those who didn't (see earlier sections on 'Birthday Pranks', 'Spiking Drinks', etc.)

DEALING WITH THOSE CRAPPY PRESENTS

You always get at least a few of them each birthday; those naff presents, usually from elderly relatives or especially spiteful or cheap friends; the paisley pattern socks, wholemeal wooly cardigans, Eau de Goat's Piss aftershave or perfume, etc, bloody etc.

Essential equipment for the birthday morning-after should include a gallon of petrol and a box of matches for the ritual destruction of these crappy offerings. Alternatively, if the old wrinklies piss off to bed early enough on party night, the whole lot can go on the barbecue (after you've finished cooking, unless you particularly like polyester-flavoured burgers).

THE AFTER-PARTY CLEAN-UP

Should have done it last night before you went to bed, shouldn't you. Ooh! Language!!

Okay, so here's what you should have done: Hire a steam-hose beforehand, ready for the morning-after. Believe us, nothing else will even start to shift the kinds of indescribable stains you're likely to find on your carpet after the average birthday party.

Also excellent for sluicing out unwelcome overnight guests who can prove equally difficult to remove from your carpet the morning after.

In severe cases, after an especially successful party, you may feel that you might just as well chuck the carpets onto the already blazing bonfire of crappy birthday presents (see earlier section, but take care to remove sleeping guests first). And next time be sure to buy sitting room carpet with a fag-burn and wine-stain pattern.

SPONSORSHIP

This book has been officially sponsored by the National Association of Miserable Sods and Sad Bastards.

Try answering the following questions, and you may qualify for honorary membership free of charge!

Does the idea of growing older scare the shit out of you?

Would you rather everyone forgot about your birthday?

Do you think birthday parties and/or birthday presents are a waste of time and money?

Do you hate getting stupid birthday cards that are just a wasteful rip-off at over a quid for a bit of card and an envelope?

Would you prefer to be left alone to grow old and die lonely and friendless with no-one to love you?

If you answered 'yes' to three or more questions, then you qualify for free life membership of the National Association of Miserable Sods and Sad Bastards (no, the initials don't spell out anything interesting! Why should they? That's just the kind of stupid and pointless thing we hate in NAMSSB!)

To apply for membership, complete the following form.

TO: The sad bastard who sits in the corner of the pub on Sunday nights dunking his crisps in his half of bitter, heckling the domino players and muttering resentful remarks about everything under the sun.

CAN I JOIN YOU? Oh God! I'd rather shoot myself in the head!

NAME: ....

ADDRESS ....
....
....